THE INERRANCY OF SCRIPTURE

AN OVERVIEW AND DEFENSE

L. J. ANDERSON

CONTENTS

To Scott,

Thank you for being an amazing father
and supporting me in all my endeavors.

PREFACE

The book you are reading is the result of scholarly research presented in a format accessible to the general public. Normally, a work like this would not be published in this form. It would almost certainly appear as a journal article—technically accessible, but realistically out of reach for most Christians. This is simply because very few Christians who haven't attended Bible college read academic journal articles in their pursuit of God. However, many do read books.

Even pastors often find it difficult to engage with journal articles regularly, though they may have a large collection of books. Presenting research in book form, similar in depth and length to a journal article, means it can potentially reach a much broader audience. That is why virtually all of my journal-length writings are, or will be, published as short books. My goal is to provide solid academic research without requiring readers to locate or gain access to academic journals.

Additionally, I hope more authors and scholars will join me in this endeavor. Independent publishing offers many benefits and only a few significant drawbacks—namely, the lack of peer review and brand recognition. Until an author becomes well-known, they often depend on the credibility of the publisher's name. Peer review, for its part, plays an important role in academic publishing, acting as a gatekeeper to prevent poor scholarship from reaching publication.

However, peer review does not guarantee high-quality work, just as the absence of peer review does not necessarily imply poor quality. In many ways, true peer review begins after publication, when the broader academic community has the opportunity to evaluate and respond to the work. If that's the case, then an independently published book or article can undergo "organic" peer review through scholarly engagement and public critique, just like any traditionally published book provided it gains the necessary visibility.

While still largely untested, this publishing model shows promise as an alternative method of making academic research accessible. The majority of scholars continue to view independent publishing as significantly inferior to peer-reviewed articles or works released by traditional academic presses.

ABSTRACT

The Inerrancy of Scripture offers a systematic and theological examination of the doctrine of biblical inerrancy, arguing for its necessity within orthodox Christian faith. Beginning with definitions and distinctions between inerrancy and infallibility, the study surveys historical and contemporary positions, including total, limited, and no-inerrancy views. L. J. Anderson contends that the Bible's own claims about its divine origin, coupled with scriptural affirmations of God's unchanging and truthful nature, demand an acceptance of total inerrancy. The book also engages with key objections, such as the charge of circular reasoning, and addresses epistemological implications, particularly the risk of doctrinal erosion when inerrancy is rejected. Drawing on biblical texts, theological scholarship, and logical reasoning, the work concludes that affirming the inerrancy of Scripture is essential to maintaining the integrity of Christian doctrine and resisting theological compromise.

CHAPTER ONE

INTRODUCTION

T HE GENERAL ARGUMENT PRESENTED in this book was originally published as a chapter in my earlier work, *Contending for the Truth: A Biblical Look at Thirteen Contentious Doctrines*. However, I soon realized I had made a mistake in how that material was organized.

Typically, when essays are compiled into a single volume, they either share a common topic or have been published elsewhere individually. I did neither. I published them together as a single book, but the essays were unrelated in topic—connected only by their contentious nature. This presented a problem.

For instance, if someone were searching for content on the doctrine of inerrancy, they would likely never come across *Contending for the Truth*, despite it containing a dedicated chapter on the subject. The metadata simply couldn't support that many unrelated topics under one title. As a result, several solid arguments I had written on specific issues remained effectively hidden from the readers who might be looking for them.

To address this, I decided to make those chapters available individually, so that each could stand on its own and be more easily found.

This particular volume—*The Inerrancy of Scripture*—delves into an important doctrine regarding Scripture. But just how important is it? Is it an essential part of the faith? Can Christians reasonably disagree over this doctrine and still maintain an orthodox faith? These are the types of questions this book will address. Additionally, this book takes a more deductive approach to inerrancy.[1]

Brief Overview of the Debate

Before diving into the meat of the discussion, it is worthwhile to give an overview of the history of the debate on inerrancy and give an idea of just how important the debate is. While some have viewed the Bible as having

---

1. Craig Blomberg, *Can We Still Believe the Bible? An Evangelical Engagement with Contemporary Questions* (Grand Rapids, MI: Brazos Press, 2014), 122.

errors for thousands of years, the general view of the Bible has been one of its absolute authority and infallibility.[2] The debate over inerrancy really came to a head during and after the Enlightenment when reason and empirical data became king rather than God's Word.[3] To be sure, while this debate has been raging for roughly the last three centuries, the idea behind the doctrine itself is not new.[4] That said, as science started to "prove" that the Bible contained errors in regard to science or history many felt the need to reduce the Bible's authority, at least in some areas, to make it agree better with what science was saying. On the flip side, many held staunchly to the fact that the Bible is *God's* Word and thus cannot reasonably contain error.[5] The lat-

---

2. Vern S. Poythress, *Inerrancy and the Gospels: A God-Centered Approach to the Challenges of Harmonization* (Wheaton, IL: Crossway, 2012), 14.

3. Lesly F. Massey, "Biblical Inerrancy: An Anxious Reaction to Perceived Threat," *Pennsylvania Literary Journal* 13, no. 1 (Spring, 2021): 100-01, https://www.progquest.com/scholarly-journals/biblical-inerrancy-anxious-reaction-perceived-docview/2536820699/se-2.

4. John M. Frame, "Inerrancy: A Place to Live," *Journal of the Evangelical Theological Society* 57, no.1 (03, 2014): 29.

5. Keith L. Johnson, *Theology as Discipleship* (Downers Grove, IL: Inter-Varsity Press, 2015), 77.

ter have sought out various explanations for how portions of God's Word can be fully true yet possibly disagree with what science is teaching.

Importance of the Debate

There are few things more important than this debate. What is at stake in this debate is nothing less than God's nature.[6] That is not to say that God's nature may change based on this debate. Rather, man's understanding of his nature is what is at stake. How can we believe that God is who he says he is and does what he says he does if we believe that his very Word is full of errors? Also, how can we become more Christ-like and godly if the Bible may or may not reveal a true picture of who God and Christ are? In addition to providing an overview of what inerrancy is and how it is similar or different to infallibility, this volume will argue that not only is the doctrine of the inerrancy of Scripture true, but it is also necessary for Christians to hold to in order to avoid apostasy.

---

6. For a good overview of the importance of inerrancy see *Vital Issues in the Inerrancy Debate*, edited by F. David Farnell, Norman L. Geisler, Joseph M. Holden, William C. Roach, and Phil Fernandes (Eugene, OR: Wipf &Stock Publishers, 2015), 20-23.

CHAPTER TWO

OVERVIEW OF THE TERMS "INERRANCY" AND "INFALLIBILITY"

INERRANCY AND INFALLIBILITY MAY seem to be the same terms or even may seem to be unnecessary terms to some people. To be sure, these *are* theological terms for something that could be explained another way; however, they are good terms for describing the Bible. Additionally, we cannot truly address the inerrancy of Scripture unless we first understand the similarities and differences between these words.

Infallibility

Infallibility is the first term to be looked at as it is the earlier term of the two. Before "inerrancy" began being used, "infallibility" was the term of choice for theologians.

What Is Infallibility?

Infallibility is an interesting word. From a base mean-

ing of something not being fallible or able to fail, it seems
to be essentially the same word as inerrant (without error).[1] This is precisely how it used to be used. Infallibility used to be used to say that all of God's Word cannot
fail. However, as attacks on inerrancy have happened, it
has changed a bit depending on who is using the word.
For some, like me, infallibility and inerrancy remain in-
terchangeable terms, though with a slight nuance which
will be addressed fully later. That said, right now the main
thing to know is that infallibility deals with *possibility*.
Specifically, if Scripture is to be called "infallible" it cannot
have the *possibility* of failing, otherwise it is not infallible.
This is based on a simple definition of the word itself
without theological nuance being added in.

Is It Sufficient on Its Own?

The answer to this question is, unfortunately, an un-
satisfying "yes and no" because it depends entirely on what
a person means when they say God's Word is infallible.
To make matters worse, this can be very challenging to
determine. For example, I have had several conversations

---

1. Daniel J. Treier and Walter A. Elwell, eds, *Evangelical Dictionary of
Theology* (Grand Rapids, MI: Baker Academic, 2017), 791.

with Mormons. I often found these conversations to be thoroughly frustrating because the same words would be used to describe two totally different things. When a Mormon talks about "Jesus" they are not talking about the same Jesus that I am talking about. This results in a lot of talking past one another. Similarly, when some people use infallible/infallibility on their own to describe Scripture, they mean precisely what the basic meaning of the word is. In this case, yes, infallibility is sufficient by itself as it has the same basic meaning as inerrant. Others, when they talk about infallibility, do so with a different definition or idea about what infallibility is or what it applies to. In these cases, it is almost always *insufficient* because these others add in qualifiers that allow much of Scripture to be considered fallible in some regard.

Inerrancy

Inerrancy, the second word to be addressed, is necessary to engage with for a couple of reasons. First, it is technically the subject of this chapter. Second it is also the term that is most highly debated between the two. Many churches, organizations, and Christians uphold "infallibility" while simultaneously rejecting "inerrancy."

What Is Inerrancy?

Inerrancy, as already mentioned, is having no errors. To say that God's Word is inerrant is to say that, in its original manuscripts, it has no errors and is fully truthful in all that it claims.[2] However, in the same way that infallibility is sometimes used in ways outside of its basic meaning, inerrancy can also mean different things based on who is using it.[3] These differences will be looked at more in the next major section of this chapter.

How Inerrancy and Infallibility Interact

There is a nuanced difference between infallibility and inerrancy. As shown above, infallibility has to do with whether something *can* fail. Inerrancy, on the other hand, deals with whether something *did* fail. This nuance is significant even though it may not appear so. Take this book for example. It is entirely possible, however unlikely, that this book is free of all errors and is fully truthful in all its claims. Thus, while it is doubtful, this document can le-

---

2. Gregg R. Allison, *The Baker Compact Dictionary of Theological Terms* (Grand Rapids, MI: Baker Books, 2016), 79.

3. Millard Erikson, *Christian Theology* (Grand Rapids, MI: Baker Academic, 2013), 191.

gitimately be *inerrant*. That said, it can never be infallible. This is because I, being the author of the book, am not infallible. Thus, even if the book itself is inerrant, it is *not* infallible as there is the *possibility*, based on the author, that it can fail. In the case of Scripture, inerrancy is the natural outpouring of God's infallibility. God *is* infallible. He cannot err. Therefore, his Word is likewise infallible and thus inerrant.

To illustrate this a bit more, one can look at the church creeds and tradition. Why do Protestants reject the authority of the creeds and tradition, or at least place Scripture's authority above them? While it is true that most Protestants hold Scripture above the creeds and traditions, there are some who seem to be reverting back to upholding the tradition as equal to, or above, Scripture. See, for example, Kevin Giles' *The Eternal Generation of the Son: Maintaining Orthodoxy in Trinitarian Theology*. Specifically in Chapter two, Giles argues *for* the tradition as an effective means of interpreting Scripture. He argues that this does not negate the doctrine of sola scriptura (Scripture alone); however, I would argue that he has essentially fallen back into the Catholic or Greek Orthodox way of viewing the tradition (to include the creeds).

Even his book's title argues for this. Instead of looking at what Scripture says, he seems to be intent on maintaining "orthodoxy," meaning the traditional orthodox position as opposed to the biblical one. The tradition can be helpful in determining what Scripture is saying, but it should never be taken uncritically. Any tradition that goes against Scripture ought to be rejected. It is precisely the above distinction between how inerrancy and infallibility work that gives the reasoning for why we should uphold Scripture above the creeds. Any given Creed or tradition can legitimately be *inerrant,* but *none* of them can claim infallibility as they are all the product of human thinking. Now, if the tradition or Creed is firmly rooted in God's inspired Word, then it can be upheld in a similar way to God's Word. However, this is simply because they are in direct agreement with Scripture and do not have any special authority of their own.

CHAPTER THREE

OVERVIEW OF THE MAJOR DIFFERENT VIEWS ON INERRANCY

THERE ARE A NUMBER of views on "inerrancy" that must be defined. No inerrancy, limited inerrancy, and total inerrancy are the ones we will look at, though there are others.

No Inerrancy

This is a simple one. Basically, those who hold the view of "no inerrancy" do not believe that the Bible is inerrant at all.[1] This typically comes in the form of looking only at the human authors of Scripture and noting, correctly, that all humans are fallible and make errors. How-

---

1. Wynne Carlton, "Inerrancy is Not Enough: A Lesson in Epistemology from Clark Pinnock on Scripture," *Unio cum Christo* 2, no. 2 (October 2016): 68. This is also an interesting look into someone who once held to inerrancy but later rejected it.

ever, the Bible is not merely a creation by man despite what the historical-critical method of interpreting Scripture might try to suggest.[2]

Sometimes those who hold to no inerrancy simply say that it is an irrelevant doctrine. The main argument here is that this doctrine distracts from what actually matters.[3] Some even go so far as to declare the doctrine of inerrancy as the "worst heresy that has ever afflicted the Church, and it is an evil from which the Church must repent."[4] This last one is admittedly an extreme view, but it does fit under the no inerrancy category.

Limited Inerrancy

Unlike the no inerrancy camp, the limited inerrancy camp is more difficult to discuss succinctly. From a very broad perspective, it means what it means—some of the Bible is inerrant and some of it is not. However, what exactly someone who holds to limited inerrancy believes

---

2. See, for example, 1 Peter 1:20-21.

3. R. Albert Mohler, et al., *Five Views on Biblical Inerrancy*, eds. J. Merrick and Stephen M. Garrett (Grand Rapids, MI: Zondervan, 2013), 146.

4. Rodger L. Cragun, *The Ultimate Heresy: The Doctrine of Biblical Inerrancy* (Eugene, OR: Wipf & Stock Publishers, 2018), xviii.

about what is inerrant and what is not is not as simple of a question. For example, some would say that it is only inerrant in areas of faith and practice but is not in all other areas, such as scientific or historical claims.[5] Regardless of the precise view, the main takeaway is that limited inerrantists *limit* inerrancy in some way. As will be discussed in a later chapter, the limited inerrancy position has a distinct problem in that its proponents need to apply something foreign to the text of Scripture in order to determine what counts as "inerrant."

Total Inerrancy

True total inerrancy is best exemplified by the "Chicago Statement on Biblical Inerrancy."[6] This large statement on inerrancy basically states that Scripture is without error in the original documents and is fully truthful regarding everything it says. Since this is an absolute statement, adherents of total inerrancy need to explain exactly what this means. Does this mean that the original documents had

---

5. Wayne Grudem, *Systematic Theology: An Introduction to Biblical Doctrine* (Grand Rapids, MI: Zondervan Academic, 2020), 88.

6. "The Chicago Statement on Biblical Inerrancy," *Evangelical Review of Theology*, 4, no.1 (1980).

perfect grammar? Does it mean that the Bible can never record a lie? Does the Bible need to be scientifically precise as science is viewed today? Total inerrantists need to have answers to these, and similar, questions. That said, pick up a book on inerrancy or systematic theology and you will almost always find a robust defense of what total inerrancy actually entails. Total inerrancy has also been divided into multiple levels, namely absolute inerrancy and full inerrancy.[7] The difference is that an absolute inerrantist views Scripture as being fully scientifically accurate and thus must be able to explain any apparent discrepancies while a full inerrantist would argue that many of these things are just how they appear to the human eye rather than being scientifically based facts.[8] One important thing to remember is that genre plays a distinct role in this. The Bible has different genres that need to be taken into account in some way. On this, Kevin Vanhoozer says, "Two biblical passages may not be inerrant in exactly the same way; that is, not every biblical statement must state historical truth. Inerrancy must be construed broadly enough

---

7. Erikson, *Christian Theology*, 191.

8. Ibid. See Erikson's molten pool example.

to encompass the truth expressed in Scripture's poetry, romances, proverbs, parables, as well as histories."[9] While I may not like how this is phrased exactly, it does point out an important part of the Bible and a challenge that needs to be kept in mind as one seeks to interpret Scripture. Vanhoozer brings up yet another consideration of the total inerrancy view when he states, "The Bible's witness to its subject matter is always true; the interpreter's witness to the text, by contrast, suffers from various forms of existential short-sightedness, confessional tunnel vision, and cultural myopia."[10] Just because God's Word is inerrant does not mean that our interpretation of it is.

---

9. Kevin J. Vanhoozer, "The Semantics of Biblical Literature: Truth and Scripture's Diverse Literary Forms," in D. A. Carson and John D. Woodbridge (eds.), *Hermeneutics, Authority, and Canon* (Leicester: IVP, 1986): 86.

10. Kevin J. Vanhoozer, "Lost in Interpretation? Truth, Scripture, and Hermeneutics," *Journal of the Evangelical Theological Society* 48, no. 1 (March 2005): 97, https://www.proquest.com/scholarly-journals/lost-interpretation-truth-scripture-hermeneutics1/docview/211221919/se-2.

CHAPTER FOUR

THE CLAIMS SCRIPTURE MAKES ABOUT GOD AND ITSELF REQUIRE EITHER A TOTAL REJECTION OR TOTAL ACCEPTANCE OF ITS AUTHORITY

ANAKIN SKYWALKER, WHEN HE first became Darth Vader, told Obi-Wan Kenobi, "If you're not with me, then you're my enemy!" Scripture does the same. It claims certain things that force either a total acceptance of its authority or a total rejection of the same.

What Does Scripture Say About God?

Scripture makes some very significant claims about the nature of God. For one, it commonly argues, or shows God arguing, that every word from his mouth is true and perfect. Psalm 12:6 says, "The words of Yahweh are pure words, like silver refined in a furnace on the ground, purified seven times."[1] Basically, the words of Yahweh are perfectly pure. Similarly, Proverbs 30:5 says, "Every word of God proves true; he is a shield to those who take refuge in him." God cannot tell a lie as every word that he speaks is true. On the idea that God cannot lie, Numbers 23:19 says, "God is not a man, that he should lie, or a son of man, that he should change his mind. Has he not said, and will he not do it? Or has he spoken, and will he not fulfill it?" Hebrews 6:18 argues that it is *impossible* for God to lie.

Another significant claim that Scripture makes about

---

1. All Old Testament references to the divine name are written as "Yahweh." The verses quoted in this book are from the ESV, but I am unwilling to obscure God's name to appease a tradition of men—even a tradition that began with good intentions. The most used word in the entire Bible, if one discounts pronouns and similar words, is "Yahweh." In fact, it is used nearly 7,000 times which indicates its importance. We would do well to remember to give God's name its proper weight. To not do so, is to take the name of Yahweh in vain (Exodus 20:7). This verse essentially means that we are not to make the name of Yahweh worthless. In an attempt to avoid the judgment of the third of the ten commandments, the Jews refused to speak the name of Yahweh. By doing so they made his name *worthless* because they forgot what it was. I will not make the same mistake. This is a personal conviction that I believe has significant merit. God gives great weight to his name, and I cannot go against him by lessening it.

God is that he is unchanging in his nature. One such example comes from God's own mouth. Malachi 3:6 says, "For I, Yahweh, do not change; therefore you, O sons of Jacob, are not consumed." Other examples of God's unchangeability can be seen in Psalm 102:27, Hebrews 13:8, James 1:17, etc.

God cannot lie, he is unchanging, and his words are perfect according to Scripture. This is some fantastic and profound truth but this alone does not prove anything. Thus, we need to look at what Scripture says about itself. Is it God's Word?

What Does Scripture Say About Itself?

Scripture makes significant claims about God, but what does it say about itself? For one, it claims to be *from* God. One of the most recognizable references to what Scripture says about itself is found in 2 Timothy 3:16 which says, "All Scripture is breathed out by God and profitable for teaching, for reproof, for correction, and for training in righteousness." Declaring that *all Scripture* is God-breathed clearly states the origin of Scripture; however, some have raised objections to this. For example, an important hermeneutical consideration about this verse is that it was likely referring to the Old Testament. Some argue then that it does not include the New Testament. That said, Peter said that Paul's writing was Scripture just like the Old Testament. He said, "Just as our beloved brother Paul also wrote to you according to the wisdom given him, as he does in all his letters when he speaks in them of these matters. There are some things in them that are hard to understand, which the ignorant and unstable twist to their own destruction, *as they do the other Scriptures*" (2 Peter 3:15–16, emphasis added). Thus, it is best to consider Paul's statement that all Scripture is God-breathed to include the New Testament.

Another important reference to what the Bible says regarding itself is found in 2 Peter 1:20–21 which says, "Knowing this first of all, that no prophecy of Scripture comes from someone's own interpretation. For no prophecy was ever produced by the will of man, but men spoke from God as they were carried along by the Holy Spirit." This passage says that every prophecy is from God rather than man, but that just refers to prophecies about the future, right? Not so. "Prophecy" refers to a couple of different things. It is both *foretelling* and *forthtelling* the mind or will of God. One has to do with the future while the other has to do with teaching and doing God's will in the present. All of Scripture fits under this. God is revealing himself through the writers of Scripture. A prophet tells the people what God wants them to know whether that is future-focused or present-focused.

Finally, Hebrews 4:12 says, "For the word of God is living and active, sharper than any two-edged sword, piercing to the division of soul and of spirit, of joints and of marrow, and discerning the thoughts and intentions of the heart". It is impossible for any book except a book that is from God to be considered "living and active." Additionally, the writer of Hebrews is connecting this to the fact that God is the *living God* (Hebrews 3:12). Just like God is the living God, so too is his Word living and active. God proclaims, "So shall my word be that goes out from my mouth; it shall not return to me empty, but it shall accomplish that which I purpose, and shall succeed in the thing for which I sent it" (Isaiah 55:11). These Old and New Testament verses both talk about God's Word in a way that demonstrates that it is more than just human writing that is static and unable to do anything. It is living and active like God is living and active.

While there are many other verses that can be discussed regarding this, these are sufficient to demonstrate that the Bible declares that all of Scripture is from God rather than man.

Before moving on, it is important to ask: Why is it not circular reasoning to use the Bible to defend the Bible? It is not circular reasoning because of the nature of God's Word. If God really did inspire the Bible and it is indeed without error and does not contradict itself just as God cannot contradict himself, then everything in the Bible would be in accord with the truth. This is not the case with any other book in history. Every other book, being written by fallible humans and fallible humans alone, cannot make the same claims. It *is* circular reasoning to use any other book to interpret itself as I am doing with Scripture, but it is *not* circular reasoning with the Bible.

Scripture Is Either God's Word or It Is Not

Based on what Scripture says about itself and God, it must either be a false and unreliable witness or inerrant and infallible. This is because Scripture makes the claim that it is from God inspiring the writers, with much of Scripture being claimed to have been *directly* spoken by God (with the common "thus says Yahweh" phrase). If these scriptural claims are true, then it is without a doubt God's Word. Since God cannot lie and every word from his mouth is true then God's Word, the Old and New Testaments, must necessarily be inerrant and infallible. This is simply because God himself is without error and incapable of failing. Flip it over and the same is true. If Scripture errs, it is not God's Word because he cannot fail, nor can his words err.

CHAPTER FIVE

THE DOCTRINE OF THE INERRANCY OF SCRIPTURE IS NECESSARY TO AVOID APOSTASY

SOME SUGGEST THAT THE inerrancy of Scripture is unnecessary or even heretical; however, below I will demonstrate that it is *necessary* to hold firmly to it if we wish to avoid falling in our faith.

Not Holding to Inerrancy Makes
Every Doctrine in Scripture Suspect

One of the major arguments in Stephen Andrew's article on biblical inerrancy is the epistemological argument. He states, "The argument holds that, once inerrancy is surrendered, all of Scripture becomes suspect in regards to trustworthiness."[1] Basically, if Scripture is not fully inerrant, then *every* part must be viewed as untrustworthy until it has been proven trustworthy. But who, or what, is the arbiter of truth in this case? In every instance, the arbiter of truth is *not* God's Word. Something else must be applied to Scripture to combat this. For example, the biblical account of creation has to be interpreted through the lens of science rather than the other way around. Many adherents of limited inerrancy are aware of this exact problem. However, the solution is often to elevate their own minds, their reason, as being the arbiter of truth on whether specific passages are inerrant.[2] Obviously, there is a distinct danger here. If one's mind or reason determines whether a passage is inerrant, then it is only a matter of time until relativism rears its ugly head, and personal beliefs begin to twist Scripture in ways it was never meant to be twisted. This leads directly to the next argument.

The "Slippery Slope" Argument

The slippery slope argument is essentially that, once

---

1. Stephen L. Andrew, "Biblical Inerrancy," *Chafer Theological Seminary Journal* 8.1 (Winter 2002): 10.

2. Andrew, "Biblical Inerrancy," 17.

the inerrancy of Scripture is rejected, the person, group of people, or organization that rejected it would slip away from orthodoxy. The logic is simple. If God's Word is not held as inerrant and infallible by the person studying it then they are liable to twist Scripture to their own agendas rather than let Scripture teach them. Some insist that the slippery slope argument needs not to be used because it is not guaranteed. For example, Stephen Andrew points out that Fuller Theological Seminary removed "inerrancy" from their statement of faith roughly seventy years ago and has not since slipped into unorthodoxy.[3] Unfortunately, this is a lack of understanding of what constitutes "falling from orthodoxy." While Fuller has not made any additional changes to their statement of faith, they *have* demonstrated significant breaches in orthodoxy. This can readily be seen in some of the classes offered, the professors and their teachings, and how these things have affected

---

3. Ibid., 10.

4. For example, C. Peter Wagner taught for approximately 30 years at Fuller while his teachings both there and outside of Fuller have had a massive impact and much of that is outside of orthodoxy. Additionally, I have personally seen a church descend into unorthodoxy based on the teachings of other Fuller professors.

churches.[4] On one occasion, this resulted in a backlash prompting Fuller to remove a class from their registry only to reinstate it a year later with less emphasis on it.[5] Additionally, Fuller recently made a significant change to their stance on LGBTQ ideology. While their "official" stance has been maintained, the school's position notes that "'faithful Christians' can hold other views."[6] It is clear that, even when the "official" stance of a group or organization is still in line with orthodoxy (sans inerrancy), the slippery slope is a real thing that needs to be argued in the case of someone rejecting inerrancy.

---

4. For example, C. Peter Wagner taught for approximately 30 years at Fuller while his teachings both there and outside of Fuller have had a massive impact and much of that is outside of orthodoxy. Additionally, I have personally seen a church descend into unorthodoxy based on the teachings of other Fuller professors.

5. Alister McGrath, *Christianity's Dangerous Idea: The Protestant Revolution—A History from the Sixteenth Century to the Twenty-First* (New York, NY: HarperCollins Publishers, 2007), 419.

6. Daniel Silliman, "Fuller Seminary Reaffirms Historic LGBTQ Stance," *Christianity Today*, May 23, 2025, accessed June 8, 2025. https://www.christianitytoday.com/2025/05/fuller-seminary-reaffirm-lgbtq-sexuality-marriage-stance/

CHAPTER SIX

CONCLUSION

THE DOCTRINE OF THE inerrancy of Scripture is an extremely important topic. Satan and the world want nothing more than for Christians to water down the truth in God's Word to the point where entire sections of Scripture are rejected as being myth or merely culturally subjective. Strikingly, the most significant threat often comes not from outside the church, but from within. It is fellow believers in Christ. Yet, this is not entirely unexpected. Scripture is clear that the biggest threats to true faith are those who come from within as wolves in sheep's clothing and well-meaning but misguided believers. A high view of the doctrine of inerrancy is necessary to combat many of the attacks that have come against Scripture and the church in modern times.[1] Part of this is recognizing that total inerrancy is the view that most accurately aligns with God and his Word. God does not lie, nor does he change. Every word from his mouth is true and the Bible is *his* Word. This needs to be held to staunchly, otherwise, we are liable to fall into unorthodoxy.[2]

---

1. Gregory K. Beale, *The Erosion of Inerrancy in Evangelicalism: Responding to New Challenges to Biblical Authority* (Wheaton, IL: Crossway Books, 2008), 17. Beale gives two possibilities as to why inerrancy is being eroded in evangelical circles.

2. John MacArthur, ed., *The Inerrant Word: Biblical, Historical, Theological, and Pastoral Perspectives* (Wheaton, IL: Crossway, 2016), 1.

A Brief Call to Action

If you found value in this book, please consider leaving an honest review on your favorite book review site (Amazon, BookBub, Goodreads, etc.). Reviews are tremendously helpful to authors. They are, in many ways, the lifeblood of a book and I highly appreciate each one that I receive.

Also, if you are interested in receiving updates on books, book reviews, and other short teachings that I publish, you can follow me on:

- Facebook (Meta): L. J. Anderson at www.facebook.com/profile.php?id=61553506423559

- YouTube: L. J. Anderson at www.youtube.com/@ljandersonbooks

- My website: www.ljandersonbooks.com

ALSO BY L. J. ANDERSON

Books

- *Contending for the Truth: A Biblical Look at Thirteen Contentious Doctrines*

Short Books

- *Theology and Apologetics: An Examination of How and Where They Intersect*

- *The Moral Argument: Is It Worth Having in Your Apologetic Repertoire?*

- *Scientific Naturalism and Old Earth Creationism: Are They More Reasonable Alternatives to a Young Earth?* (coming soon!)

- *Gnosticism: A Biblical and Historical Response* (coming soon!)

BIBLIOGRAPHY

Allison, Gregg R. *The Baker Compact Dictionary of Theological Terms*. Grand Rapids, MI: Baker Books, 2016.

Anderson, L. J. *Contending for the Truth: A Biblical Look at Thirteen Contentious Doctrines*. Billings, MT: Lamad Press, 2025.

Andrew, Stephen L. "Biblical Inerrancy." *Chafer Theological Seminary Journal* 8.1 (Winter 2002): 1-20.

Beale, Gregory K. *The Erosion of Inerrancy in Evangelicalism: Responding to New Challenges to Biblical Authority*. Wheaton, IL: Crossway Books, 2008.

Blomberg, Craig. *Can We Still Believe the Bible? An Evangelical Engagement with Contemporary Ques-*

tions. Grand Rapids, MI: Brazos Press, 2014.

Carlton, Wynne. "Inerrancy is Not Enough: A Lesson in Epistemology from Clark Pinnock on Scripture." *Unio cum Christo* 2, no. 2 (October 2016): 67-81.

Cragun, Rodger L. *The Ultimate Heresy: The Doctrine of Biblical Inerrancy.* Eugene, OR: Wipf & Stock Publishers, 2018.

Erikson, Millard. *Christian Theology.* Grand Rapids, MI: Baker Academic, 2013.

Frame, John M. "Inerrancy: A Place to Live." *Journal of the Evangelical Theological Society* 57, no.1 (03, 2014): 29-39.

Giles, Kevin. *The Eternal Generation of the Son: Maintaining Orthodoxy in Trinitarian Theology.* Downers Grove, IL: IVP Academic, 2012.

Grudem, Wayne. *Systematic Theology: An Introduction to Biblical Doctrine.* Grand Rapids, MI: Zondervan

Academic, 2020.

Johnson, Keith L. *Theology as Discipleship.* Downers Grove, IL: InterVarsity Press, 2015.

MacArthur, John, ed. *The Inerrant Word: Biblical, Historical, Theological, and Pastoral Perspectives.* Wheaton, IL: Crossway, 2016.

Massey, Lesley F. "Biblical Inerrancy: An Anxious Reaction to Perceived Threat." *Pennsylvania Literary Journal* 13, no. 1 (Spring, 2021): 100-120, 342.

McGrath, Alister. *Christianity's Dangerous Idea: The Protestant Revolution—A History from the Sixteenth Century to the Twenty-First.* New York, NY: Harper-Collins Publishers, 2007.

Mohler, R. Albert, et al. *Five Views on Biblical Inerrancy*, eds. J. Merrick and Stephen M. Garrett. Grand Rapids, MI: Zondervan, 2013.

Poythress, Vern S. *Inerrancy and the Gospels: A God-Cen-*

tered Approach to the Challenges of Harmonization.
Wheaton, IL: Crossway, 2012.

Silliman, Daniel. "Fuller Seminary Reaffirms Historic
LGBTQ Stance." *Christianity Today.* May 23, 2025.
Accessed June 8, 2025.

"The Chicago Statement on Biblical Inerrancy." *Evangelical Review of Theology,* 4, no.1 (1980).

Treier, Daniel J., and Walter A. Elwell, eds. *Evangelical Dictionary of Theology.* Grand Rapids, MI: Baker
Academic, 2017.

Vanhoozer, Kevin J. "Lost in Interpretation? Truth, Scripture, and Hermeneutics." *Journal of the Evangelical Theological Society* 48, no. 1 (March 2005): 89-114.

Vanhoozer, Kevin J. "The Semantics of Biblical Literature: Truth and Scripture's Diverse Literary Forms."
in D. A. Carson and John D. Woodbridge (eds.),
Hermeneutics, Authority, and Canon (Leicester: IVP,
1986): 49-104.